MAKING
"GOOD OF THE ORDER"
THE BEST
PART OF YOUR
MEETINGS

HOW TO IMPROVE MORALE, TEAMWORK & CREATE A MORE POSITIVE ENVIRONMENT ONE MEETING AT A TIME.

LISA GIRUZZI & ROBBIE MACCUE

A publication of 911 Leadership Books
@911Leadership

Cover Design & Production assistance by Amy Bennett

ISBN:-10: 0692632387

ISBN-13: 9780692632383

LISA GIRUZZI & ROBBIE MACCUE

DEDICATION

We dedicate this book to all the Emergency Responders who give their lives to save others, who run in when others are running away, who make a meaningful difference every single day and to their leaders.

Thank you all very much.

CONTENTS

LISA GIRUZZI & ROBBIE MACCUE

ACKNOWLEDGMENTS

We would like to acknowledge all the leaders we have encountered in our lives for being willing to reach higher, demand more and be the change they wished to see in the world.

You have inspired us.

INTRODUCTION

"Perhaps those who are best suited to power are those who have never sought it. Those who ... have leadership thrust upon them, and take up the mantle because they must, and find to their own surprise that they wear it well."
~J.K. Rowlings, Author

As someone who started out young in the EMS industry and was thrust into a leadership position, I look back over the last decade and think of the many lessons learned along the way.

When elected president of an EMS organization at the age of 20, I was often faced with many challenges and opportunities. Some opportunities were missed and others were created.

Whether you are reading this book as a leader or someone who wants to positively influence the current leadership or culture of your organization, you're in the right place. **Remember, leadership is more than just a position.**

How did I survive over 10 years? I never gave up and, more importantly, I grew up. As challenging as it was at times, I persevered, although I admit writing numerous resignation letters over the years that I never submitted. Many people came along with me on this journey, left an imprint on my life and kept me on the path.

In leading well over 100 organizational meetings, I now see how easy it is to go with the flow and do what has always been done to get by. In some cases it may just be treading water to survive as an organization or survive the membership and the many opposing personalities that come with it. One opportunity that is rarely leveraged and often overlooked is the "good of the order" section of the meeting.

Roberts Rules of Order is a popular publication giving recommendations for how meetings should be run. In the publication *Roberts Rules for Dummies*, they define "Good of the Order" as the last part of a meeting agenda:

> *This is a time set aside for members to offer comments or observations (without formal motions) about the society and its work. The good of the order is also the time to offer a resolution to bring a disciplinary charge against a member for offenses committed outside of a meeting.*

Wow. Read that again. Would you really want your meetings to end on everyone giving their opinion of the organization or bringing up others on disciplinary charges? It's no wonder people don't want to come to another meeting if that's what they have to look forward to.

Often members would mention that Sally Sue was sick and argue over a fruit basket or sending a card (it's a more reoccurring conversation that pops up over the years than you would think).

For many years I just sped through this part of the meeting, as many organizations do, and missed opportunities to create lasting positive change. I began to realize that this was an opportunity to positively impact the way people felt as they left the meeting. No matter what is said or discussed during the meeting, often it is what happens at the end of the meeting that they will carry with them and remember.

I, with the help of Lisa Giruzzi, began creating and experimenting with different exercises and conversations to have during the "Good of the Order." I was delighted to find that people participated enthusiastically and even came up with good ideas. Even the people I least expected to participate (you know the ones - the curmudgeons who are quick to come up with a negative comment) were eager to join in.

THE FORMAT & WHAT TO EXPECT

We have formulated, created and practiced the 12 activities included in this book and have experienced great results. Attendance at monthly meetings has increased and the members are much more collaborative in their participation. Members are now leaving the organizational meeting with an upbeat attitude instead of scratching their head and contemplating how they will never get that last hour or two of their lives back. Instead of rushing out of the building like their hair's on fire, members leave smiling and talking about high-point experiences or excited about what they will take on next to impact the community.

While I cannot attribute all of the positive changes in my organization to doing the exercises in this book, this was a crucial piece of the puzzle to creating a thriving organization. By doing lots of little things, we saw lots of big changes

"Little hinges swing big doors." - Jim Rohn

Each of the chapters in this book is an activity that can be led in front of your group. Each activity is designed to take approximately 10 minutes or less.

It's helpful to remember that your organization did not get into the state that it is in overnight. It will take some work to rectify. Remember: patience is a virtue. As a leader it is also important to remember that causing positive change in an organization, or a transformation as we like to call it, is best accomplished by thinking of it as an elephant. Yes, an elephant! How do you eat an elephant? (No, this is not a joke). One bite at a time.

Each exercise is designed to take a bite out of your elephant, and little by little change can begin to happen.

CREATING AN INTRO

How to introduce this new concept to your meetings.

"All truth passes through three stages. First, it is ridiculed. Second, it is violently opposed. Third, it is accepted as being self-evident."
~ Arthur Schopenhauer

If you are like most people, you might have a concern about introducing something new or doing something this different in your organization especially since most organizations have a tendency towards negativity. That is natural.

Each one of these exercises on its own has the potential to positively impact the culture of your organization. Taken together, month after month they can truly make a big difference. Think of the exercises as building blocks towards a better future.

Let us share the story of "Sarah" who attended one of our Leadership Training Programs. Prior to coming to our EMS Leadership Academy training, Sarah had taken on a leadership position in her volunteer EMS organization. The organization was in a great deal of turmoil. Sarah was committed to turning things around by figuring out how to stop the destructive attitudes and building a stronger more cohesive team. Despite her best efforts, things were not getting better. In fact, she overheard members of her organization calling her "The Dictator." Sarah was distraught when she came to us and didn't know what to do next. Through participating in EMS Leadership Academy programs, she gained many insights and ideas for how to positively impact her organization.

One action she decided to experiment with right away was using the "Good of the Order" for a positive, engaging activity at her upcoming member meeting. She was nervous to say the least, as her previous efforts were not successful. Despite her concerns, she created an exercise declaring her commitment and vision for the organization. She requested each member in attendance at the meeting write down one thing he or she appreciated about the organization. Here is the exercise she created:

As the Chief of this organization, I am committed to developing myself and being the best leader I can be. I am also committed that our organization be the best it can be and I know you are committed to that too. Although we are facing problems there is a lot that works about our organization.

Please write in the space below what you are most proud of about our organization: _____
_____
_____

She collected the slips of paper and read them out loud at the end of the meeting. To her amazement all of the comments but one were extremely positive. As she read each of the comments out loud, she noticed the impact on the group. People were smiling and there was a more positive atmosphere. It was a turning point for Sarah as a leader and for the organization. When people shifted from focusing on what was wrong to what they appreciated, it reminded people why they were there; it reignited their passion for the work of the organization and gave them the opportunity to stand for what they believed in.

It is very easy to go with the flow of complaints, commiserate and be negative. Anyone can do that. A leader on the other hand is someone who stands up and declares that something else is possible even when it doesn't look that way. A leader interrupts the status quo and creates a new future. Sarah is a true leader and her organization is reaping the benefits of her leadership.

7

Don't discount the power of each of these exercises!

"Life changes when you focus on what's working."
~Lisa Giruzzi

So, how do you introduce the exercises?
Just do the exercise and don't talk about it.

Engaging in the exercise is what matters, not what you say about it or how you describe it. Just give them the instructions, i.e. tell them what to do. They will follow your lead. Be firm and direct them. Trust us, it will all turn out!!

A few notes about the exercises:

* ❖ The exercises do not have to be done in the order we laid them out. If you want to be really creative, put the numbers 1 through 12 in a hat and draw one out each month and do the corresponding exercise. You can't get this wrong. As Nike® says… "Just do it!"

* ❖ At the bottom of each page is an opportunity for you to track the success of each exercise. First, rate yourself on a scale of 1 to 10 with "1" being not effective and "10" being extremely effective. In other words, think objectively: How did people participate? Did you get the result you were hoping for? How comfortable were you with delivering the exercise? This is not an opportunity to beat yourself up. It is an opportunity to learn from the exercise. Also, there is a place to track the number of attendees at the meeting. Lastly, there are two questions for you to answer. It is helpful to have the first question in mind as you are leading the exercise. Look for what's working about the exercise. You will be amazed at

what you see. Then after it is all over, ask yourself how you can improve for next time. Leaders are not afraid to look at their performance and learn from it.

❖ In some of the exercises we have added a "Bonus Exercise" that is optional. The intention of the Bonus Exercises is to give people the opportunity to spread the positivity in between meetings to those who were not in attendance and to keep the insights from the meetings alive beyond the meeting.

❖ Have fun! These exercises are an effort to unleash the natural creativity and enthusiasm of the participants. In our experience that happens best in an environment of fun and play. Seriousness and criticism DO NOT foster creativity. Most often, when an organization is not thriving, what's missing is creativity and innovation. That becomes available in the space of fun. Don't take our word for it! Test it for yourself.

❖ The handout for each exercise is provided in the appendices so that you can make copies of it to distribute to the attendees. It is ok for you to reproduce the handout for use at the meeting for the purposes of the activity.

❖ Each exercise has an intention and a rationale provided so that you have an understanding and background about the activity. You can read them out loud to the group or not. It's up to you. Trust your judgment.

EXERCISE #1
WHAT ARE YOU PROUD OF?

Intention of Exercise:

    To give the people attending the meeting the opportunity to share their proudest moments.

Rationale:

    Organizations thrive when the members are engaged and enthusiastic about the organization. Encouraging members to share their proudest moments creates an environment where positivity and enthusiasm are welcomed.

Supplies You'll Need:
- Copies of handout - Appendix A
- Pens/pencils

Action Steps / Activity:

1. Pass out handout to each participant.

2. Each person writes on handout the three (3) things they are most proud of about being a member of the organization.

3. Ask everyone to find a partner.

4. Everyone shares with their partner the three things they wrote down on the handout. Read your own list out loud to the group then ask, "Who would like to share with us your list of what you are most proud of?" Allow 2 to 3 people to share their list. **IMPORTANT:** Manage the rest of the group during the sharing. Do NOT allow any negative comments, wisecracks, etc. The person sharing is taking a risk and it is your job to keep it safe for them to share.

5. Thank people for engaging in the exercise.

Bonus Assignment: (Optional)

Invite members to engage in a bonus assignment. Between now and the next meeting ask 3 to 5 other members of the organization what they are most proud of about the organization and share your list with them.

Tracking & Rating:

1 to 10 _____

# of Attendees at Meeting: _____

What worked about this?

How can I improve upon this next time?

EXERCISE #2
SUCCESS LEAVES CLUES

Intention of Exercise:
> To focus on something that worked and see what there is to learn.

Rationale:
> What we focus on we get more of. Our greatest potential for learning is in our areas of strength not in our weakness. When you recognize and acknowledge what works about you, your members and your organization you will begin to see everything differently, which will spark innovative thinking and whole new possibilities for action. This is the environment that allows the best in people to emerge.

Supplies You'll Need:
- Copies of handout - Appendix <u>B</u>
- Pens/pencils

Action Steps / Activity:

1. Ask everyone to find a partner. Pick an "A" and a "B" to see who will go first.

2. Pass out handout to each participant.

3. Have partner "A" interview partner "B" using the questions on the handout. After 3 minutes ask partners to switch so that partner "B" interviews partner "A". Allow 3 minutes for the second interview (total 6 minutes).

4. Ask, "Who would like to share what you learned from the interview? **IMPORTANT:** Manage the rest of the group during the sharing. Do NOT allow any negative comments, wisecracks, etc. The person sharing is taking a risk and it is your job to keep it safe for them to share.

5. Take note of the enthusiasm and positivity in the room.

6. Thank people for engaging in the exercise.

Bonus Assignment: (Optional)

Ask people to notice how they feel when talking about a highpoint experience. Invite them to use the handout to interview someone who is not in attendance at the meeting tonight prior to the next meeting.

Tracking & Rating:
1 to 10 _____

# of Attendees at Meeting: _____

What worked about this?

How can I improve upon this next time?

EXERCISE #3
LETTING GO OF THE PAST

Intention of Exercise:

>To think differently about the past so that it is not a barrier to the future being fulfilled.

Rationale:

>Building your organization by focusing on the past is like trying to drive your car forward looking in your rearview mirror. It doesn't work well. Most organizations spend way too much time either trying to avoid past mistakes or reliving the "glory days" trying to get back there. We are not suggesting that you ignore the past, only that you put it in its place: behind you so it's not in your way.

Supplies You'll Need:
- Copies of Handout - Appendix <u>C</u>
- Pens/pencils

Action Steps / Activity:
1. Inform the group that they will be engaging in an exercise and they will **<u>NOT</u>** be asked to share what they write with anyone.

2. Pass out handouts.

3. Read question #1 from handout out loud. Ask people to write their answer to question #1 on their handout. Give 3 minutes for this part of the exercise.

4. Read question #2 from handout out loud. Ask people to write their answer to question #2 on their handout. Give 3 minutes for this part of the exercise.

5. Ask people to make note of what they see out of this exercise on the back of their handout. Give 2 minutes for people to reflect on anything they learned.

6. Thank people for engaging in the exercise.

Tracking & Rating:
1 to 10 _____

# of Attendees at Meeting: _____

What worked about this?

How can I improve upon this next time?

EXERCISE #4
GETTING TO KNOW YOU

Intention of Exercise :

For members to learn something new about other members of the organization.

Rationale:

Studies show that when individuals feel connected and have a sense of belonging to a group they tend to stay with the organization longer as well as demonstrate increased levels of performance.

Supplies You'll Need:
- Copies of handout - Appendix D
- Pens/pencils

Action Steps / Activity:

1. Pass out handout to each attendee.

2. Give the attendees 1 minute to answer the 2 questions on the handout.

3. Ask each attendee to share their answer to both questions on handout with a partner. (1 to 2 minutes)

4. Have each attendee stand up and share one thing they learned about their partner. NOTE: This is a quick share, "One thing I learned about Bill is _____." It helps if the leader demonstrates how to do it prior to asking the group to do it.

5. Thank the group for engaging in the exercise.

Bonus Assignment: (Optional)
Invite participants to use the handout to interview a member of the organization who is not in attendance at the meeting tonight.

Tracking & Rating:
1 to 10 _____

# of Attendees at Meeting: _____

What worked about this?

How can I improve upon this next time?

EXERCISE #5
ATTITUDES ARE CONTAGIOUS

Intention of Exercise :

> To discover how our attitudes influence others intentionally and unintentionally and how to change from a negative to a positive attitude.

Rationale:

> **"It is our attitude at the beginning of a difficult task**
> **which, more than anything else, will affect**
> **its successful outcome." - William James**

> Often we notice other people's negative attitudes but we fail to be aware of our own and the impact it has on others. Awareness is the first step to change. In order to create a thriving organization, members need to be conscious of their attitude and its impact on others.

Supplies You'll Need:
- Copies of handout - Appendix <u>E</u>
- Newsprint paper and easel or whiteboard
- Markers

Action Steps / Activity:
1. Introduction: Everyone knows that being around negativity is no fun and can be detrimental to morale and productivity but not everyone knows how to change their attitude (mood) when they feel stuck.

2. Ask everyone to find a partner.

3. Pass out handout.

4. Have each person share with their partner the answer to question #1 on the handout (3 minutes total).

5. Brainstorm* a list of ideas of how to shift your attitude from negative to positive. Ask for a volunteer to write people's answers on the newsprint paper or whiteboard as people shout out responses (Examples: Listen to music, meditate, exercise, talk to a friend, etc.).
   Brainstorm means to create a list of ideas from the audience where there are NO WRONG answers. It is to incite creativity and generate new ideas.

6. Ask attendees to pick 1 or 2 ideas from the list and experiment with using them over the next month. In other words, when they notice they are in a bad mood or have a negative attitude use one of the ideas from the list to change their attitude.

7. Ask someone to be accountable for copying the list and distributing it (via email or other means) to all the attendees within 1 to 2 days.

Tracking & Rating:

1 to 10 _____

# of Attendees at Meeting: ____

What worked about this?

How can I improve upon
this next time?

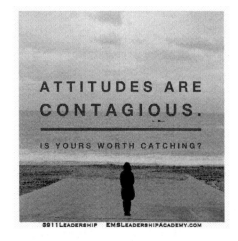

ATTITUDES ARE
CONGAGIOUS.

IS YOURS WORTH CATCHING?

@911LEADERSHIP   EMSLEADERSHIPACADEMY.COM

EXERCISE #6
INTEGRITY & ACCOUNTABILITY

Intention of Exercise:

To broach the subject of Integrity as the foundation for "workability."

Rationale:

Integrity is the foundation for workability. Integrity is a term that most people equate with honesty and morality and it is seen as a "fixed" state, i.e., either you have integrity or you don't. What if instead integrity had more to do with honoring your word? Said another way, to have integrity means that you "walk your talk," i.e., your words and your deeds (actions) match. The most effective organizations have a foundation for integrity and accountability as part of the fabric of the organization.

Supplies You'll Need:

- Handout - Appendix F - A copy of the article Michael Jensen interview entitled, "Integrity: Without it Nothing Works".

  http://bit.ly/1PZJmfN (Use this link, then click on "download this paper" button. Note: you can download it anonymously without creating an account).

Action Steps / Activity:

1. Prior to the meeting, read the article on Integrity and highlight the sections that you want read during the meeting. Optional: Identify someone who will be attending the meeting and who is well respected. Request that they read the

article prior to the meeting and commit to reading parts of the article out loud at the meeting.

2. Inform the audience that during the Good of the Order we will be reading an article together on Integrity because it is the source of extraordinary performance and everyone in the room is committed to extraordinary performance. The most important thing while listening to the article being read is to listen for how you can get to this next level of performance. Where is your integrity "out" and what can you do about it.

3. After the article is read, ask for 1 or 2 people to share any insights or ideas that the article sparked.

4. Distribute the link to the article and invite people to read it again for themselves prior to the next meeting.

Tracking & Rating:
1 to 10 _____

# of Attendees at Meeting: _____

What worked about this?

How can I improve upon this next time?

EXERCISE #7
TIME TO CELEBRATE

Intention of Exercise:

> To give attendees an opportunity to value their own contribution and the contribution of others to the organization.

Rationale:

> Celebrating wins and acknowledging people's success reinforces that they matter. You get more of what you reward.

Supplies You'll Need:

- Copies of handout - Appendix <u>G</u>
- Pens/pencils

Action Steps / Activity:

1. Pass out handout to each attendee.

2. Ask everyone find a partner. Pick an "A" and a "B" to see who will go first. NOTE: This exercise works best if you partner with someone that you don't know as well.

3. Have partner "A" interview partner "B" using the questions on the handout. After 2-3 minutes ask partners to switch so that partner "B" interviews partner "A". Allow 2- 3 minutes for the second interview (total 6 minutes).

4. Ask, "Who would like to share what you learned from the interview? **IMPORTANT**: Manage the rest of the group during the sharing. Do NOT allow any negative comments,

wisecracks, etc. The person sharing is taking a risk and it is your job to keep it safe for them to share.

5. Take note of the enthusiasm and positivity in the room.

6. Thank people for engaging in the exercise.

Bonus Assignment: (Optional)

Ask people to notice how they feel when talking about what they value most and engaging in a positive conversation. Invite them to use the handout to interview someone who is not in attendance at the meeting prior to the next meeting.

Tracking & Rating:
1 to 10 _____

# of Attendees at Meeting: _____

What worked about this?

How can I improve upon this next time?

EXERCISE #8
A NEW FUTURE

Intention of Exercise:

To get out of the box that constrains and limits future accomplishments and begin to imagine a new future for the organization. The main point is to get the creative juices flowing.

Rationale:

"A vivid image of the future compels the whole body."
~ Aristotle

Having a hopeful, positive image of the future impacts your actions in the present. By gathering input from everyone in the room about what their ideal future would look like for the organization it begins the conversation for what's possible and takes the attention off "what's wrong" or "why not." It triggers a different part of the brain and allows for new innovative ideas to emerge.

Supplies You'll Need:
* Copies of handout - Appendix H
* Sticky / Post-It Notes® & Marker

Action Steps / Activity:
1. Pass out handout to each attendee

2. Read the question on the handout aloud to the audience.

3. Ask attendees to shout out answers. Write each item or idea they say on a sticky note and place the sticky note on the wall. Keep asking, "What else? If you did not have to worry about 'the how,' what would you want to see?" NOTE: If

someone says an idea such as "a new station," DO NOT react, just write it down on a sticky note and post it on the wall. Continue to solicit ideas from the audience and post them on the wall.

4. After everyone has finished, ask what is present for people out of doing the exercise. Notice if people are energized or not.

5. OPTIONAL: Ask for a few volunteers to organize the sticky notes into categories such as Facility, Personnel, Equipment, etc. or any other way the notes could be organized.

6. OPTIONAL: Ask people to "vote" (by a raise of hands?) on the one or two ideas that they think should be the first priority. Ask for volunteers to start researching the best way to achieve the one with the most votes.

7. REMEMBER: The point of this exercise is to stimulate ideas and to get people talking about a positive future. It is not necessarily about accomplishing any of the items and that might be an outcome of the exercise.

8. Thank the attendees for participating in the activity.

Tracking & Rating:

1 to 10 _____

# of Attendees at Meeting: ____

What worked about this?

How can I improve upon this next time?

The best way to predict the future is to create it
-Peter Drucker

EXERCISE #9
COMMITING TO EXCELLENCE

Intention of Exercise:

> For everyone in attendance at the meeting to get on the same page regarding excellence.

Rationale:

> Everyone has a different meaning of what the word "Excellence" means. In fact, Google has over 290 million search results for that word. Chances are each person in the room also has a different definition as well. Getting on the same page regarding excellence will help people to practice it and recognize it when they see it.

Supplies You'll Need:

- Copies of the handout - Appendix I
- Newsprint with easel or Whiteboard
- Markers

Action Steps / Activity:

1. Pass out handout to each attendee.

2. Ask everyone to find a partner. Pick an "A" and a "B" to see who will go first.

3. Have partner "A" interview partner "B" using the questions on the handout. After 2 minutes ask partners to switch so that partner "B" interviews partner "A." Allow 2 minutes for the second interview (total 4 minutes).

4. Take sharing from audience and create a list of the "core factors" that define excellence and write each answer on the

newsprint or whiteboard.

5. Thank everyone for participating in the exercise.

    Bonus Assignment: (Optional)

    Ask attendees to pick 1 or 2 items from the list to focus on over the next month and practice it to increase excellence in the organization. What are you willing to commit to in order to enhance the excellence of our organization?

Tracking & Rating:
1 to 10 _____

# of Attendees at Meeting: _____

What worked about this?

How can I improve upon this next time?

EXERCISE #10
ACKNOWLEDGEMENT & APPRECIATION

Intention of Exercise:

> To acknowledge and appreciate the members for the difference they are making in the community and the world.

Rationale:

**A person who feels appreciated will
always do more than is expected.**

Each of us has a strong desire to make a difference in the world and one of the ways we can confirm the difference we make is by being acknowledged and or appreciated for it. Most folks who work or volunteer in the EMS industry are not doing it for the accolades or recognition however, it is critical that people feel appreciated in order for them to continue to perform at such high levels. This "job" is too hard to do day in and day out without recognizing how much of a difference you are making.

Supplies You'll Need:

- Copies of handout - Appendix J
- Pens/pencils

Action Steps / Activity:

1. Read the Rationale from above out loud to the group. NOTE: Many people are uncomfortable receiving appreciation, so you have to be willing to confront the attendees un-comfortableness with understanding and still gently push them to participate in the exercise.

2. Pass out handout to each participant.

3. Ask everyone to find a partner. Pick an "A" and a "B" to see who will go first. Have partner "A" interview partner "B" using the questions on the handout. After 2 minutes ask partners to switch so that partner "B" interviews partner "A". Allow 2 minutes for the second interview (total 4 minutes).

4. Ask people to publically acknowledge or appreciate someone in the room. IMPORTANT: Manage the rest of the group during the sharing. Do NOT allow any negative comments, wisecracks, etc. The person sharing is taking a risk and it is your job to keep it safe for them to share.

5. Thank everyone for participating in the exercise and for attending the meeting. Acknowledge the difference they are making in the lives of community members.

6. OPTIONAL: Share a recent positive story that illustrates the contribution of the organization to the community.

    Bonus Assignment: (Optional)

    Ask the attendees to make a commitment to acknowledge and appreciate each other and other members of the organization over the next month. Request that if someone acknowledges or appreciates you for something you did respond with, "Thank you," and leave the story or deflection out.

Tracking & Rating:
1 to 10 _____
# of Attendees at Meeting: _____
What worked about this?
How can I improve upon this next time?

EXERCISE #11
POSITIVE IMPACT OF PARTICIPATION

Intention of Exercise:

　　To acknowledge the positive impact of their participation in this organization on the rest of their lives.

Rationale:

　　When individuals recognize the reciprocal relationship they have with the organization it shifts the mindset from "helping out," i.e. doing the organization a favor, to a mindset of "mutual contribution," i.e. they are getting as much out of their participation as they are giving. This shift in mindset makes a huge difference in the nature of people's participation especially when people are considering taking on a leadership role.

Supplies You'll Need:

- Copies of the handout - Appendix K
- Newsprint with easel or Whiteboard
- Markers

Action Steps / Activity:

1. Pass out handout to each attendee.

2. Ask everyone to find a partner. Pick an "A" and a "B" to see who will go first.

3. Have partner "A" interview partner "B" using the questions on the handout. After 2 minutes ask partners to switch so that partner "B" interviews partner "A". Allow 2 minutes for the second interview. (total 4 minutes).

4. Take sharing from audience and create a list of the ways being a member of the organization has positively impacted or contributed to the member's life. **IMPORTANT**: Manage the rest of the group during the sharing. Do NOT allow any negative comments, wisecracks, etc. The person sharing is taking a risk and it is your job to keep it safe for them to share.

5. Thank everyone for participating in the exercise.

Tracking & Rating:
1 to 10 _____

# of Attendees at Meeting: _____

What worked about this?

How can I improve upon this next time?

EXERCISE #12
BE THE CHANGE

Intention of Exercise:

> To help members discover that the best access to making a positive difference in the organization (and the world) is to first and foremost alter their way of being and acting.

> **"Be the change you wish to see in the world."**
> **~Gandhi**

Rationale:

> Our ways of being communicate louder than any other form of communication we use. "Being" trumps speaking and action every time. Think about the last time you saw someone slamming things around yet when asked what's wrong they reply loudly, "NOTHING!" What do you believe - their way of being or what they say? Our way of being has an enormous impact on the world around us and by being responsible for it and being willing to change it we can cause any change we want to see within the organization. Attitudes are contagious. Choose the one you want to spread.

Supplies You'll Need:
- Copies of handout - Appendix L
- Pens/pencils

Action Steps / Activity:
1. Read the Rationale (above) out loud to the group.

2. Invite people to consider that we all have ways of being that are helpful/positive and that we also have some that are unhelpful/negative. If each of us became aware of our ways

of being that are destructive/unhelpful and committed to changing these ways of being we could cause a transformation in our organization.

3. Pass out the handout to each attendee. Inform them that sharing from this exercise will be voluntary.

4. Give the attendees 4-5 minutes to answer the questions on the handout.

5. Invite people to share what they discovered out of participating in the exercise. **IMPORTANT:** Manage the rest of the group during the sharing. Do NOT allow any negative comments, wisecracks, etc. The person sharing is taking a risk and it is your job to keep it safe for them to share.

6. Thank people for engaging in the exercise.

Bonus Assignment: (Optional)
Ask attendees to pick 1 way of being from their list to focus on over the next month and practice it to "Be The Change" in the organization. Ask, "What can we count on from you to cause a positive change in our organization?"

Tracking & Rating:
1 to 10 _____

# of Attendees at Meeting: _____

What worked about this?

How can I improve upon this next time?

CONCLUSION

"It's not the critic who counts;
not the man who points out how the strong
man stumbles or where the doer of deeds
could have done them better. The credit
belongs to the person who is in the arena.
Whose face is marred with dust and sweat and
blood; who strives valiantly ... who at the best
knows in the end the triumph of high
achievement, and who at the worst, if he fails,
at least fails while daring greatly."
~Dr. Brené Brown recounting a speech by President
Theodore Roosevelt

The world is full of critics and cynics sitting "in the stands," while you the leader are in action every day "on the court" of life. Just by reading this book we know you are a leader and your organization (and the world) has a brighter future. There is hope of overcoming the naysayers and spectators in the stands. We hope you have the courage to take a stand, to make a difference and persevere.

As Lisa and I developed communication and leadership training for the EMS industry, and formed the EMS Leadership Academy, many outspoken critics exclaimed that "this is just positive thinking," "you can't change people's behavior" or "people should be happy that they're making a difference by helping people, why do they need to be told?"

For all of those people, it is a true story for them, and there is no arguing with their reality. They have created a self fulfilling prophecy where change is not possible, and curiously they do not offer a different solution. However, for those leaders we have worked with and those organizations that have put our advice into action, they have benefitted greatly and have discovered for themselves that positive change is in fact possible.

It's worth repeating that your organization did not get to its current state overnight, and it will take consistent actions over time to change the culture.

Remember the secret to eating an elephant:
   it's one bite at a time.

For more information visit:

www.EMSLeadershipAcademy.com

APPENDICES

APPENDIX A

Exercise # 1 Handout

Make a list of three (3) things that you are most proud of regarding being a member of our organization (examples included accomplishments, successes, personal growth, etc.).

1)

2)

3)

APPENDIX B

Exercise # 2 Handout

Reflecting back over your time here at <u>Organization's name</u> you've certainly had, as we all have, high points and low points.

Tonight I would like you to focus on a high point experience; a time when you felt enlivened, energized, engaged, excited and/or fulfilled. Tell the story of the highpoint experience to your partner. Give details such as when it happened, who was involved, challenges you overcame, what you learned, etc.

What was it about **you** that made the high-point experience possible?

What was it about the **situation** that brought out your best?

APPENDIX C

Exercise #3 Handout

1. Reflect back over your past experience with this organization. If there was one thing you wish didn't happen or one thing you would like to change, what would it be and why?

2. Make a list of 5 good things that resulted from what happened or the way it happened, i.e. you learned something, you connected with someone, etc.:

   a. _____

   b. _____

   c. _____

   d. _____

   e. _____

3. What opened up for you out of this exercise?

APPENDIX D

Exercise #4 Handout

What I like most about being a member of this organization is:

_____

_____

_____

_____

One thing you might be surprised to know about me is:

_____

_____

_____

_____

APPENDIX E

Exercise #5 Handout

We all know that being around negativity is no fun and can be detrimental to morale and productivity but not everyone knows how to change his or her attitude (mood) when feeling stuck.

1. Think about a time in the past when you were upset, frustrated or had a negative attitude and you were able to shift to a more positive outlook. What helped you to shift your perspective? What technique or strategy helps you to turn your attitude around?

APPENDIX F

Exercise #6 Handout

Article: Integrity: Without it Nothing Works

Link: http://bit.ly/1PZJmfN

(Use this link, then click on "download this paper" button. Note: you can download it anonymously without creating an account).

APPENDIX G

Exercise #7 Handout

1. How long have you been with the organization?

2. What attracted you to join or be a part of this organization?

3. Without being humble, share what you value most about your work here in this organization.

4. What are the qualities, characteristics or strengths that you bring to this organization?

APPENDIX H

Exercise #8 Handout

Imagine tonight you fall asleep and when you awake it is five years in the future and our organization has changed in all the ways you most want it to as if by magic. What would you like to see in this future?

APPENDIX I

Exercise #9 Handout

1. Reflect back over your personal and professional experiences and tell a story of a time that stands out for you as an example of excellence.

2. In your opinion, what are the core factors necessary for excellence to occur? In other words, what does excellence look like?

APPENDIX J

Exercise #10 Handout

1. Tell me a story of a time when you felt truly appreciated for something you did?

2. What do you want to be acknowledged for regarding your participation in this organization?

3. *(Read this to your partner)* I really appreciate you and your contribution to this organization. I want to acknowledge you for _____
_____. *(their answer to question #2. Look them in the eye as you acknowledge them.)*

APPENDIX K

Exercise #11 Handout

1. How has being a member of this organization positively impacted the rest of your life? In other words, what are you now able to do now that you couldn't do before joining?

2. What are the top 2 ways you have grown as a person since being a member here?

APPENDIX L

Exercise #12 Handout

1. What do I see is missing from the organization that I want to see more of (this is not a tangible thing like money or new equipment. Examples might include teamwork, positive atmosphere, appreciation, etc.)?

2. What way or ways of being do I now have that act as a barrier to having the results I want (from question #1)?

3. Think of someone you admire. What way(s) of being do they have that helps them to be successful?

4. What way of being can I adopt to cause the change I want to see?

5. What is the first step I will take to begin practicing the change I want to be?

About the Academy

Our purpose is to be the source of transformational leadership in Emergency Services. We empower leaders to cause other leaders and to create bold visions that redefine the future of their organization and Emergency Services worldwide. Our work causes lasting, sustainable, positive change.

EMS Leadership Academy was born out of a collaboration between Robbie MacCue and Lisa Giruzzi after they worked together to produce miraculous results at the non-profit ambulance organization where Robbie serves as the president. After working together on this project and sharing the results, one thing became abundantly clear, the problems experienced at his organization were not unique, numerous other agencies were experiencing similar problems and were hungry for an answer.

Lisa and Robbie have combined their expertise and talents to form the EMS Leadership Academy to address the difficulties so many EMS organizations are facing on a daily basis. These difficulties include things like a dwindling membership due to the "revolving door" syndrome – where new people join just as quickly as others are leaving – and a lack of engagement of members resulting in a few dedicated, overburdened people running the organization. In addition, because there has been a shortage of meaningful, effective leadership training for EMS personnel, there is often a lack of qualified leaders to choose from to ensure a sustainable, thriving organization

This recipe for disaster leaves non-profit EMS organizations vulnerable to being dismantled and replaced by for-profit ambulance companies rather than neighbors working together, delivering a high quality of care to the residents of their town.

Lisa and Robbie are committed to changing all that with the innovative and transformational programs offered through the EMS Leadership Academy. Lisa and Robbie promise to help their clients to create a magnetic, thriving and sustainable organization.

ABOUT THE CO-FOUNDERS OF EMS LEADERSHIP ACADEMY

Lisa Giruzzi is a best-selling author, result-producing consultant and an award-winning trainer with more than twenty-five years' experience helping individuals and organizations to be more successful and achieve their goals. She specializes in causing breakthrough results for her clients by giving them access to a whole new level of power and performance.

Robbie MacCue has more than 14 years experience in the EMS industry. Currently, he is a flight paramedic with the Town of Colonie, NY. For more than 10 years, Robbie has served as President of Sand Lake Ambulance, a non-profit EMS organization in Upstate New York. In addition, Robbie is a CPR instructor who is passionate about empowering others to save more lives. He teaches physicians, nurses and Physician Assistants CPR at medical schools and hospitals throughout Manhattan with a medical training group, Medcon Associates.

To learn more visit: www.EMSLeadershipAcademy.com

A Special Invitation ...

Join our online mini-course:

Breathing New Life Into Your Organization

About this mini-course:

Given the nature of the work you do, doing more with less is adding enormous stress on everyone in your organization, especially the leaders. You do not need the added stress of interpersonal difficulties and conflict. Focusing on communication will enable your organization to transform its culture at all levels.

When you are aware of the Three Little Known Communication Strategies Guaranteed to Breathe Life into Your Organization you can begin to change the nature of the conversations in your organization, which will start you on a path to creating a magnetic organization where people will *want* to participate.

Sign Up:
http://courses.EMSLeadershipAcademy.com

Made in the USA
Columbia, SC
29 September 2020